Auntee Edna

Written by Ethel Footman Smothers
Illustrated by Wil Clay

EERDMANS BOOKS FOR YOUNG READERS

Grand Rapids, Michigan / Cambridge, U. K.

To my grandchildren:
Ryan, Keila, Raquel, Jaye, Ashly, Victoria, and Tyler.
I hope you will always love books — and each other.
With special thanks to
Peggy Bradberry, Telisa Mayfield, and Charlene Smith
— E. F. S.

To Kirby Elizabeth Richardson, who modeled for
most of the illustrations, and to her very supportive
parents, Julie and Gaylord Richardson.
— W. C.

Text ©2001 by Ethel Footman Smothers
Illustrations ©2001 by Wil Clay

Published 2001 by Eerdmans Books for Young Readers
An imprint of Wm. B. Eerdmans Publishing Co.
255 Jefferson Ave. SE
Grand Rapids, Michigan 49503
P.O. Box 103, Cambridge CB3 9PU U.K.

www.eerdmans.com/youngreaders

Printed in Hong Kong
01 02 03 04 05 06 07   7 6 5 4 3 2 1

Library of Congress Cataloging-in-Publication Data
Smothers, Ethel Footman.
Auntee Edna / written by Ethel Smothers ; illustrated by Wil Clay.
p. cm.
Summary: Although at first Tokee is unhappy having to spend the day with her old-fashioned
Auntee Edna, she soon discovers her aunt is full of good ideas for fun, from baking teacakes to
putting paper rollers in their hair.
ISBN 0-8028-5154-1 (cloth : alk. paper)
[1. Aunts–Fiction. 2. Cake–Fiction. 3. Baking–Fiction.]
I. Clay, Wil, ill. II. Title.
PZ7.S66475Au 1999
[Fic]–dc21
98-49252
CIP
AC

The illustrations were done in acrylics on canvas.
The text type was set in Frys Baskerville.
The display type was set in Hollyweird.
The book was designed by Gayle Brown.

Tokee was having one of those days. Her "wish I'd never been born" kind. For no good reason Mom had said she and Reba had to stay overnight here at Auntee Edna's.

"You need to get to know your people. And don't call your auntee old-fashioned!" Mom had cautioned.

But Tokee knew Auntee Edna was old-fashioned. She didn't even have a TV. Tokee knew from the start, even before she walked through the door, that this day was going to be "stale." Tokee always said "stale" when she was bored. When she was having a "wish I'd never been born" day. And this was definitely one of those days.

Tokee's fingers played hopscotch on Auntee's couch. "Stale," Tokee thought again. "Stale. Stale. Stale."

Just then she heard Reba in the kitchen. Tokee jumped up, glad her sister was back. At least Reba would be some company. Reba had run an errand down the street for Auntee Edna. Tokee wasn't allowed. All the while Reba just went on her merry way.

"You doing something, Tokee?" Reba asked, putting Auntee's basket on the table.

"Like what?" Tokee stretched her eyes toward the ceiling. As if there was something to do in this old place. No TV. Just a big, fat nothing.

Then Tokee got an idea. "I got it. You and I could play . . ."

"That won't work. Won't work at all," an unfamiliar voice cut in. "That's strictly out of the question."

"Say what?" Tokee whirled around. And there was this screechy-eyed girl coming into her auntee's house telling her what to do.

"Say what?" Tokee said again. "You talking to me?"

"Reba and I made other plans," this other person told her. Tokee cut her eyes at Reba.

"Geraldine here is Mrs. Walker's niece," Reba tried to explain. "You know, the lady Auntee had me take those things to. Auntee says it's okay for me to go to Geraldine's for a while."

"But I thought we would do something together."

"We will, Tokee. When I get back."

"But I want to . . ."

Tokee hushed in the middle of her sentence and
tightened her lip. How come she had to be the one
cooped up here with old-fashioned Auntee Edna?
What was she supposed to do now?

"I've got a taste for some baked goods. An extra
hand would help get it done in a jiffy." Auntee Edna had
appeared as quietly as an evening shadow. She spoke as
if she had actually heard Tokee thinking.

"Need to satisfy my sweet tooth," said Auntee Edna, handing Tokee a bowl without even giving her a chance to say if she wanted to help or not.

Now Auntee would probably make her bake dinky, old cookies, thought Tokee. Stale. Stale. Stale. Auntee Edna should know by now that people don't make cookies. They buy them at the store.

"You know," her auntee said, reaching for a mixing bowl, "these won't be plain, ordinary cookies. Come to think of it, they're not really cookies at all."

"In fact," Auntee went on, "they're teacakes. Resemble a cookie, but no cookie can compare to my teacakes. Just make your taste buds jump up and shout."

Auntee Edna held each word an extra long time, letting them roll out like she was tasting some teacakes right then.

One by one Auntee named what she needed. Said she didn't need any recipe written down. Had it all tucked away in her head.

"Eggs," she called out. "I remember when we had to gather them from the hen house."

"Stale," Tokee thought and passed Auntee the carton.

"Fetch the flour now, Tokee," Auntee said. "Did you know flour used to come in cloth sacks? My mama used to sew us clothes out of those sacks."

Tokee didn't care much how things used to be, but Auntee told her anyway.

"Need some butter now." Auntee plopped a chunk in the bowl. "I churned many kegs of butter in my day. Had to milk the cow first though."

"My papa had the stubbornest cow I ever had the misfortune of knowing. But I wasn't about to let her get the best of me. I made up my mind to milk her one way or the other. Well, Maybelle, that was our cow," Auntee talked over the rim of her glasses, "Maybelle thought otherwise. She took that hind leg and sent me sprawling. Milk and all. Gave me a knot on the side of my head the size of a goose egg."

Tokee turned her head and covered her mouth, but a laugh pushed out anyway. Auntee Edna laughed too, a deep bubbly laugh. The kind that made you want to join right in.

When Auntee caught her breath, she measured the way she usually did. A couple of cups of flour. A pinch of salt. A dash of vanilla. A sprinkle of this. And a dab of that.

Soon as a wad of dough formed, Auntee said no newfangled cookie cutter was going to shape her teacakes. She and Tokee would cut them the way she always did, with a plain old jar.

They rolled the dough out on the table until it looked like a ragged-edged map. Then Tokee turned the top of the mayonnaise jar on the flattened dough. The cut pieces pushed up into the jar and slid out round and even.

eacakes in the oven, Tokee followed Auntee to the bedroom. Tokee had a button missing, and Auntee said this was as good a time as any to stitch on another.

"Seat yourself." Auntee patted the bedcovers. She took a tin box from the closet, handed it to Tokee, and told her to "pop the lid."

Tokee opened the lid and all sorts of buttons spilled out. Dime-thin ones. Big, thick, chunky ones. Some wavy

with ridges. Some smooth and shiny like jewels. Some were
robin's egg blue. Some the color of rainy day clouds, all
dull and gray. Others were shaped like dried up leaves. Still
others were small and round like peas.

Tokee couldn't believe her eyes. "Where did these all
come from?"

"Put some away myself. Some passed on to me."

"Really?"

"M-m-m-huh." Auntee chose a button. "This one belonged to your great-great uncle who fought in the Civil War. And this one here," Auntee picked up another button, "was left by your great-great grandma who was born in 1875. She was a dressmaker. One of the first of our family to own her own business. This one's from her shop."

"For real?" Tokee's eyes widened.

"All true," Auntee said.

"Why do you keep all of them?"

Auntee bit the thread and knotted the end. "Never know when you might need one."

Tokee smiled, "Like now?"

"Like now," Auntee winked.

Then Tokee ran her hands through the button pile and held one up.

"What's this one about? Any kind of memory go with it?"

"Not in particular. Not until now." Auntee said. "Look in the basket and bring me that string."

Tokee passed Auntee the string. Auntee broke two long pieces and handed one to Tokee. "Wet the string like this." Auntee licked the end of her piece and picked up a button. "Now take your button and run the end of the string through the eyes of the button."

Tokee slipped the string through one eye and back through the other. Then she knotted the ends. Just like Auntee.

"Now take it like this," Auntee instructed.

Tokee looped the string over a finger on each hand. She twirled the string with the button in the middle until the string got all twisted and bunched together. Then she pulled like Auntee Edna did. The button whirled and whined in a blur of color. The string stretched like rubber.

"This is great." Tokee laughed. "Who taught you how to make these? What are they called?"

"Oh, we made these and lots of other playthings coming up. Some folks called this a zoo-zoo. Suppose others called it something else. No matter. Had ourselves a pretty good time just the same."

By now the house smelled vanilla sweet, and Auntee put the teacakes on the windowsill.

"What other kinds of things did you do when you were growing up?"

"Well now, when I was no bigger than a bump on a log, just like you," Auntee chuckled, "all the womenfolk used brown paper to put curls in their hair."

"Brown paper?" Tokee frowned.

"Might seem odd, but it worked."

Auntee took a paper bag, tore a long wide strip, and twisted it tight. Then she wrapped some of her hair around it and tied the paper with the ends sticking up.

"Do mine," Tokee pleaded.

Auntee Edna put paper bag rollers all over Tokee's head. Then Tokee put paper bag rollers all over Auntee Edna's head. Tokee laughed, sure she didn't look half as funny as Auntee Edna did. Like someone, the way Auntee put it, "dressed up like a porcupine."

"What's bringing on the giggles?"

Tokee laughed some more. "You."

"Oh, is that so?" Auntee chuckled and reached for a mirror so Tokee could have a look at herself.

"The aliens done landed." Reba came in the back door.

"Do I look really weird?" Tokee covered her face.

"Worse," teased Reba.

"You're back pretty early," Auntee observed. "Anything wrong?"

Reba looked at the floor and then back at Tokee.

"Geraldine and I don't think the same. I decided to come back and do something with Tokee."

"Good," Tokee said. "Then we can make you look just like us. Give you a headful of paper bag rollers, too."

Later when the shadows had grown deep, Tokee, Reba, and Auntee Edna sat on the front porch, hair in paper bag rollers, looking like porcupines and eating teacakes. They watched specks of light flicker across the yard. Lightning bugs, Auntee Edna called them. Said when she was coming up they used to catch them and put them in jars. Carried those jars around just like lanterns.

Tokee wondered what they'd do tomorrow. Old-fashioned stuff wasn't too bad after all. Neither was Auntee Edna.

Tea Cakes

1¼ cup sugar
½ cup soft butter or margarine
2 eggs
3 tablespoons vanilla
3 cups flour
¼ teaspoon salt
½ teaspoon baking soda
2 tablespoons milk

Preheat your oven to 350 degrees.

Combine sugar, butter, eggs, and vanilla in a large bowl. Mix well.

Stir together flour, salt, and baking soda in another bowl.

Alternately add the flour mixture and the milk to the sugar and butter mixture. Stir until well blended.

Form the dough into a ball. Put the dough on a floured surface and knead until dough is smooth. Sprinkle a little flour over the dough as needed to prevent it from sticking. Using a quart jar or a rolling pin, roll out the dough ½ inch thick.

Cut with a large-mouthed jar or round cookie cutter. Place on an ungreased cookie sheet. Bake for 12-15 minutes or until lightly brown. Cool and remove from cookie sheet.